Mountains

Keith Lye

Franklin Watts
London • New York • Sydney • Toronto

© 1992 Franklin Watts

Franklin Watts
96 Leonard Street
London EC2A 4RH

Franklin Watts Australia
14 Mars Road
Lane Cove
NSW 2066

UK ISBN: 0 7496 0853 6

10 9 8 7 6 5 4 3 2 1

Series Editor: A. Patricia Sechi
Editors: Ambreen Husain and
    Claire Llewellyn
Artwork: Karen Johnson
Cover artwork: Hugh Dixon
Picture research: Ambreen Husain
Education advisor: Joy Richardson

A CIP catalogue record for this book
is available from the British Library

Printed in Italy by G. Canale & C. SpA

Contents

What are mountains?

Mountains are high places which rise above the land around them. From the tops of mountains, you can look down on **plains** and valleys. Many mountains have steep rocky slopes and sharp **peaks.** They can be hard to climb. Other mountains have gentle slopes and rounded peaks. There are mountains all over the world even under the sea.

▽ Many mountains have jagged peaks.

3

What is a mountain range?

Some mountains are single peaks. Others are joined together in rows called mountain ranges. Some mountain ranges rise up from the **ocean** floor but their peaks are hidden under the water. On land, the world's highest mountain range is the Himalayas in Asia. It contains Mount Everest, the world's highest mountain.

▽ Mount Everest is nearly nine kilometres high. People first managed to climb it in 1953.

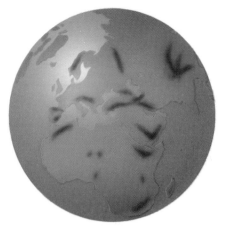

◁ Mountain ranges are found all over the world.

▽ The map shows where the biggest mountain ranges are found and what they are called.

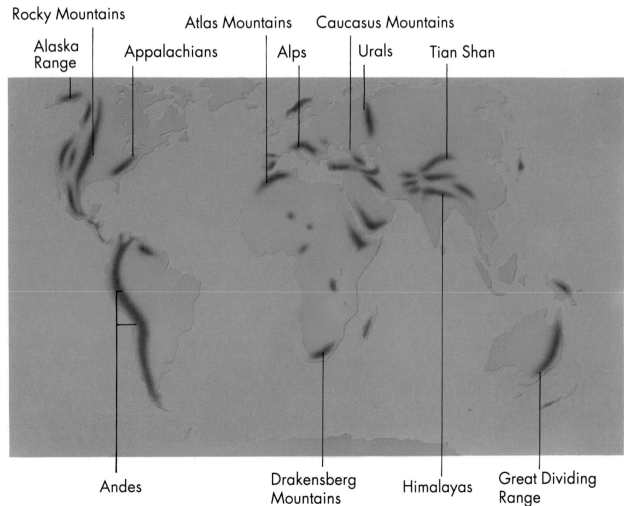

Rocky Mountains

Alaska Range

Appalachians

Atlas Mountains

Alps

Caucasus Mountains

Urals

Tian Shan

Andes

Drakensberg Mountains

Himalayas

Great Dividing Range

Fold mountains

The **earth** may seem solid and unchanging but it is not. Below the surface it is so hot that some rocks melt. The earth's surface is cooler and forms a crust. We live on this. The crust is cracked. Large pieces of it push so hard against each other that layers of rock are forced up into folds. These rise up to make 'fold mountains'.

▷ You sometimes see the folds in rocks in railway or road cuttings or in cliffs.

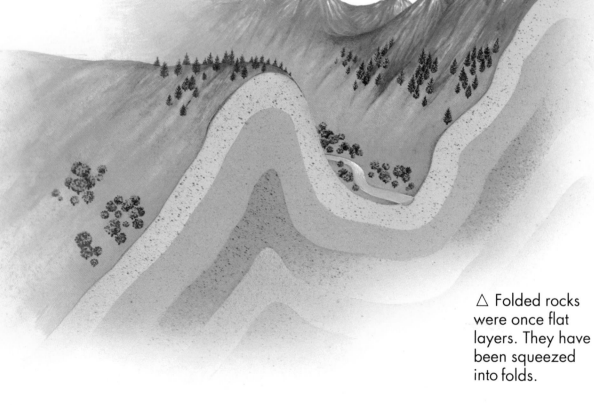

△ Folded rocks were once flat layers. They have been squeezed into folds.

Block mountains

When pieces of the earth's crust move around, the rocks often crack. Long deep cracks in the rocks are called faults. Sometimes huge blocks of land which lie on a fault are pushed up and become mountains. In the United States there are several block mountains including the Sierra Nevada range.

▽ The Sierra Nevada is a block mountain range.

▽ Block mountains form when chunks of land are pushed up along faults.

▽ Rift valleys are formed when chunks of land slip down between faults.

▷ Faults are long cracks in rocks where the rocks have moved up, down or sideways.

Exploding mountains

Not all mountains are found in ranges. Some are single mountains such as volcanoes. These are places where hot runny rock from inside the earth pours out of holes in the ground. The hot rock is called lava. Volcanoes sometimes explode hurling lava and ash into the air. Volcanoes are made from lava and ash which have piled up and hardened to form a mountain.

▷ Red-hot lava shoots out of volcanoes. This volcano is on the island of Hawaii.

▽ Some of the highest mountains are volcanic islands. They rise up from the sea-bed.

Mountain weather

Mountains change the kind of weather a place has, especially how much rain there is. Mountains can be dangerous places. Sudden storms may bring strong winds with heavy rain or snow.

   As you climb up a mountain it becomes colder. Even in hot countries the highest mountain peaks are very cold. They are always covered by snow.

▷ Mount Kilimanjaro is Africa's highest peak. It is hot at the bottom but has ice at the top.

▽ On the other side of the mountain the weather is dry. All the rain has fallen.

▷ Air is always moving over the earth. It contains some water.

▷ Tiny drops of water are carried in the wind. As it blows over a mountain clouds form and the water falls as rain.

△ Many rivers start
high up in the
mountains where the
ice slowly melts.

13

Snow and ice

Heavy falls of snow pile up in hollows on a mountainside and are pressed into solid ice. In time the ice spills out and moves slowly downhill. These rivers of ice are called **glaciers**. They are so heavy that they grind away rocks and make deep wide valleys. The top of a glacier has long deep cracks called crevasses.

▽ Glaciers are huge rivers of ice. They form high up in mountains.

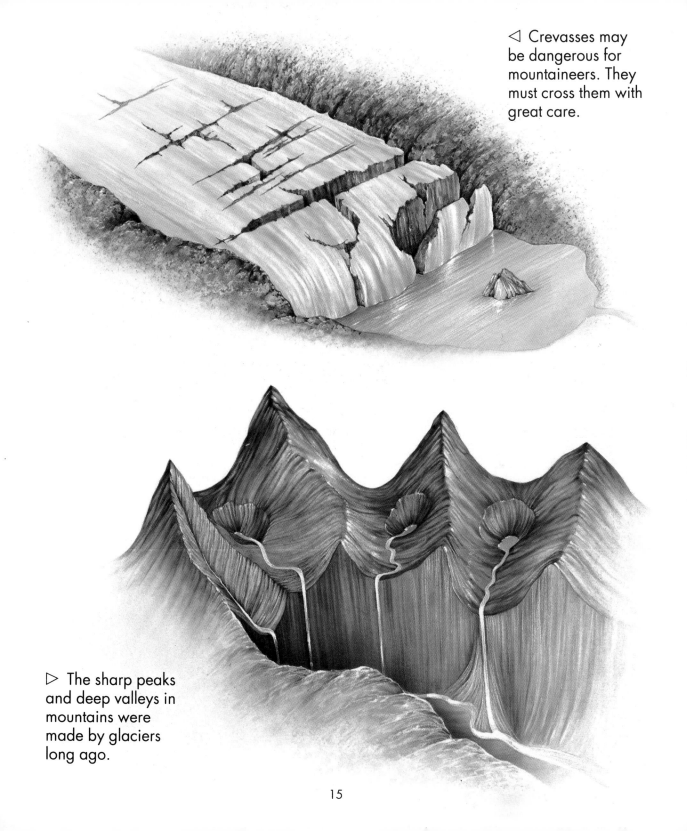

◁ Crevasses may be dangerous for mountaineers. They must cross them with great care.

▷ The sharp peaks and deep valleys in mountains were made by glaciers long ago.

Danger in the mountains

Loose snow on mountain slopes sometimes slides downhill. This often happens in spring when the snow begins to melt. A large mass of falling snow is called an avalanche. It buries everything in its path.

A landslide is another danger. This occurs when earth and rocks slide down a mountain.

▷ Avalanches of snow and rock are one of the greatest dangers in mountains.

▽ The huge waves may break the dams that hold the water. This causes flooding.

△ When rocks crash into a reservoir, a place where water is stored, huge waves are formed.

Living in the mountains

Few people live in the mountains. Travelling is not easy here and the winter weather is bad.

High up the air is very thin and has less oxygen. This is the gas we all need to live. People who live in the highest mountains have bigger **lungs** than us. They can breathe in more oxygen with each breath.

▽ Winding roads are common in mountains. The slopes are too steep for straight roads.

▽ Bridges and tunnels carry roads and railways through the mountains.

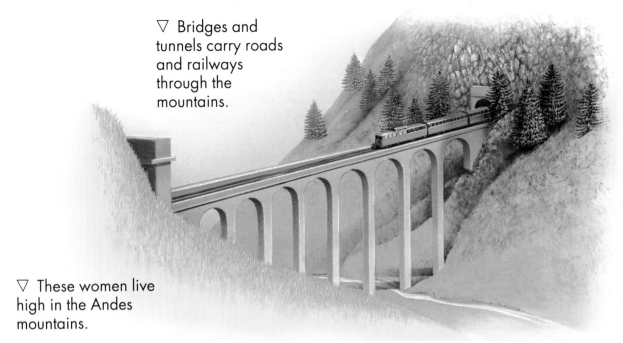

▽ These women live high in the Andes mountains.

Farming in the mountains

Farming is difficult on steep mountain slopes. Rain washes the soil away. Some farmers build fields called terraces to grow their crops. These are like huge steps on the mountain slopes.

In summer grass covers many mountain slopes. Farmers take their animals to feed on this grass.

▷ Terraces are flat areas of ground where crops grow on mountain slopes.

▽ In summer farmers take their cattle to feed on new grass high up the mountain.

Mountain riches

Wood from mountain forests is used to make many things including the paper in this book. Mountain rocks often contain **minerals** and metals such as gold and silver. Miners dig out these rocks.

Dams have been built across some mountain rivers. Lakes form behind the dams, and the water is used to drive machines that make electricity.

▷ Reservoirs are built in some mountains. The water drives machines that make electricity.

◁ Forests grow on the lower slopes of mountains. Wood from these forests is very valuable.

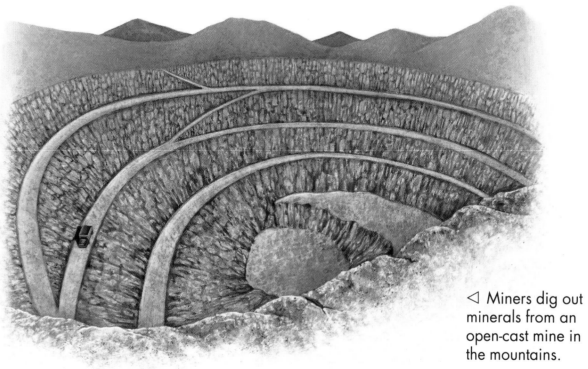

◁ Miners dig out
minerals from an
open-cast mine in
the mountains.

Mountain plants

Different plants grow at different heights on mountains. Trees only grow on the lower slopes. It is too cold and windy for them to grow on the high slopes. The highest point where trees can grow is called the tree line. Above this most plants are small and hug the ground. No plants grow on the highest, snow-covered peaks.

▷ Brightly-coloured rhododendrons grow on the lower slopes of the Himalayan mountains.

▽ Plants change as you climb up a mountain. Grassland and forests grow near the bottom of Mount Kenya in Africa. At the top there is only ice.

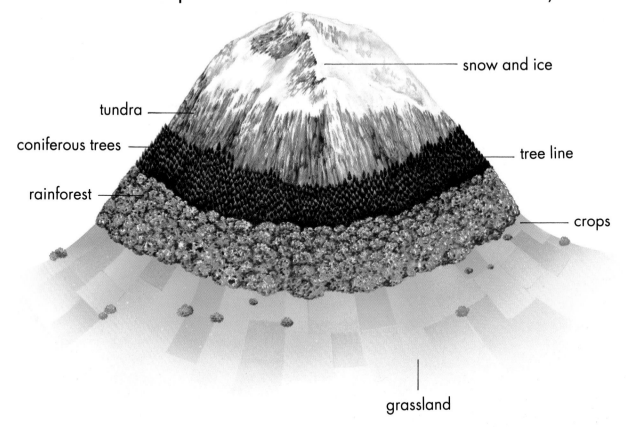

snow and ice

tundra

coniferous trees

rainforest

tree line

crops

grassland

24

▷ Moss campions grow low down in clusters. This protects them from the wind and cold.

▽ Edelweiss grows in the Alps. The fine hairs that cover it protect it from the cold.

◁ Glacier buttercups grow in high wet places in the Alps.

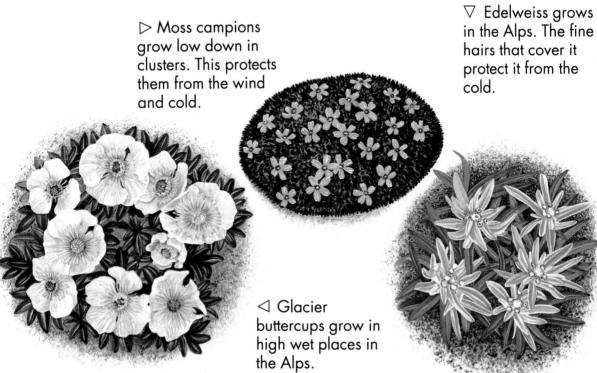

Mountain animals

Mountain animals have to be good climbers. The shape of their hooves helps them to scramble over rocky slopes as they look for grasses and other food.

Mountain animals must be able to survive the cold. Many of them have thick coats to keep warm. A few animals such as marmots sleep through the winter.

▷ Rocky Mountain sheep, or bighorns have special pads on their feet to help them climb.

▽ Yaks have thick coats to keep them warm. They live in the Himalayas.

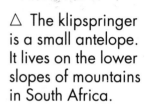

△ The klipspringer is a small antelope. It lives on the lower slopes of mountains in South Africa.

▽ The ibex is a
goat. It lives in
mountains in Europe
and Asia.

▽ The Andean
condor is a huge
vulture. It lives in the
Andes Mountains of
South America.

▷ The marmot is a
small mountain
animal. It sleeps
through the winter.

Mountain sports

Many people enjoy walking in the mountains. The scenery is beautiful and there are wonderful views. Some people like to climb the steepest slopes but for this they need special equipment. Thousands of tourists visit the mountains in winter to ski and toboggan.

▷ Mountain-climbing is an exciting but dangerous sport.

△ Skiing is very popular. Many people enjoy it in the winter months.

Facts about mountains

- The world's highest mountain is Mount Everest. It rises 8.8 kilometres above sea level.
- The volcano Mauna Kea on the island of Hawaii is even higher than Mount Everest. From its base on the ocean floor it is more than ten kilometres high, but only four kilometres of it can be seen above sea level.

Mount Aconcagua
6,959m

Mount McKinley
6,194m

Mount Kilimanjaro
5,895m

Mount Elbrus
5,633m

Mount Kosciusko
2,228m

Mount Everest
8.84m

△ If you put together the highest mountains from each part of the world they would look like this:

Glossary

cliff A very steep and high rocky slope.

crust The outer hard shell of the earth.

coniferous trees Trees which are always green and which grow cones such as firs and pines.

earth The planet on which we live. Earth is also the name for the soil in which plants grow.

glacier A river of ice which moves slowly down a mountain or across land.

lungs The organs inside our bodies that enable us to breathe.

mineral A mineral is any substance which is not alive and which can be dug out of the ground.

oceans Large areas of water that lie around the land. Oceans cover much of the earth.

peak The top of a mountain. Some peaks are pointed.

plains Areas of almost level land.

rainforest A forest where the trees are green all the time and which is very damp. Rainforests receive a lot of rain.

rocks The solid materials that form the outer part of our earth.

tundra An area high up a mountain or in the Arctic where it is cold all year round and where only small scrubby plants grow.

valley A long usually narrow area of land lying between hills or mountains.

Index

Photographic credits: Bruce Coleman Limited 17 (K Gunnar), 27 (E & P Bauer); GSF Picture Library 7, 21; Robert Harding Picture Library 4, 8 (K Francis), 14, 29 (B O'Connor); Tony Morrison South American Pictures 19; David Paterson 3, 25; Science Photo Library 7, 21; Zefa 13, 23.